Women Who Dared

by Alison Auch

✦ Table of Contents ✦

Introduction

Throughout history, outstanding men and women have worked to improve the lives of other people. Many of these men and women are known for their work as **humanitarians** (hyoo-man-ih-TARE-ee-uhns).

Humanitarians are dedicated to making life better for others. They notice when people are treated unfairly, and they bravely decide to do something about the **injustices** they see.

In order to do their work, humanitarians often need to be **activists**, too. Sometimes being an activist means getting people to see things in a new or different way. Sometimes it means placing oneself in danger in order to uphold a belief.

➤ Diana, Princess of Wales

Mohandas Gandhi ⚘

Humanitarians and activists are courageous people. They often must act in ways that make them unpopular. They need to believe strongly in their ideas for making the world a better place. Most important, they need to care deeply about others.

The people pictured on these pages were famous humanitarians. In the pages that follow, you will read about three other famous humanitarians—women who dared to work for the rights of others.

✤ Martin Luther King, Jr.

Harriet Tubman, Susan B. Anthony, and Eleanor Roosevelt are three important American women. Although they were from different backgrounds, each was a famous humanitarian and activist. The changes they made in people's lives are still part of the world in which we live today.

Harriet Tubman

Susan B. Anthony

Born enslaved, Harriet Tubman helped other slaves escape to freedom. Susan B. Anthony worked for the fair treatment of women in the United States. Eleanor Roosevelt used her influence as First Lady of the United States to make the world a better place for women and children.

Eleanor Roosevelt

✔ Point

Think It Over

Why do you think you read more about great men in U.S. history than great women? Write down your thoughts. Can you think of other women who did important things for people?

Harriet Tubman
1820 - 1913

❖State of Maryland❖

Dorchester County,
Maryland

Harriet Tubman was born into slavery. Once she became a free person, she risked her life over and over to help free other enslaved African Americans.

Harriet Tubman was born around 1820 in Dorchester County, Maryland. She was born Araminta Ross and was called "Minty" as a young girl. She began using her mother's name, Harriet, when she was older. She is known by this name today.

Harriet and her family were owned by a man named Edward Brodas. Slavery was legal in parts of the United States through much of Harriet's life. Slaves both young and old were not free to live their lives as they wished. They were forced to work for their owners.

Life was extremely difficult for Harriet and her family. They lived in a one-room cabin. They had few clothes, shoes, and blankets for warmth. Food was often scarce. The work was very hard and their owners were generally cruel to them. Slaves were not allowed to learn to read or write. Slave children did not go to school.

When Harriet was five or six, she went to work for the Cook family as a house servant. The Cooks treated her badly. Harriet became sick and had to return to the Brodas family.

As Harriet grew older, she became angry about being enslaved. She knew it was not right and wanted to do something about it.

IT'S A FACT

Slaves were often traded and sold at auctions. The person who offered the most money for a slave bought him or her. Families were often torn apart when different members were sold to different slave owners.

7

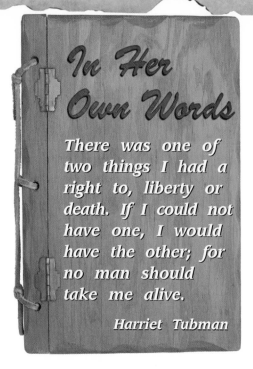

In Her Own Words

There was one of two things I had a right to, liberty or death. If I could not have one, I would have the other; for no man should take me alive.

Harriet Tubman

One day as Harriet was working outdoors, she saw a runaway slave trying to escape. A man chasing the slave wanted Harriet to stop him. Harriet refused. The man threw a heavy weight at the slave, but hit Harriet in the head instead. As a result of this injury, she suffered from headaches, blackouts, and tiredness for the rest of her life.

Harriet went to work with her father. The man they worked for allowed her to do extra jobs when her work was done. She was paid for these jobs. Little by little, Harriet began to save money. She also began to dream of freedom.

Cotton was the backbone of the South's economy. Large numbers of slaves worked in the cotton fields. ⚘

In 1844, Harriet married a free man named John Tubman. After five years of marriage, she found out that she was going to be sold. So she left and headed north, to a part of the country where she could be a free woman. She traveled at night, stopping at "safe" houses where people gave her food and shelter. This network of people who helped slaves escape to the North and to Canada was called the **Underground Railroad**. Those who guided the slaves to freedom were called **conductors.**

❧ The Underground Railroad was not a real railroad. It was a complicated network of safe houses and routes that extended into Canada.

IT'S A FACT

In 1850, Congress passed the Fugitive Slave Act, which made it a crime to help slaves who were trying to make it to freedom. The act also required that any former slaves caught in the North be returned to slavery in the South. This meant that conductors on the Underground Railroad had to get slaves to Canada in order to guarantee their freedom.

Harriet's 130-mile journey to freedom ended in Pennsylvania. She settled in the city of Philadelphia, where she found work and a place to live. Although she loved her freedom, she missed her family very much. She wanted them to join her.

Harriet joined the Philadelphia Vigilance Committee, a branch of the Underground Railroad. She learned that her sister Mary and Mary's children were trying to escape.

It was common  for slave owners to offer rewards for the capture and return of their runaway slaves.

$100 REWARD! RANAWAY

From the undersigned, living on Current River, about twelve miles above Doniphan, in Ripley County, Mo., on 2nd of March, 1860, A NE GROMAN, about 30 years old, weighs about 160 pounds; high forehead, with a scar on it; had on brown pants and coat very much worn, and an old black wool hat; shoes size No. 11.

The above reward will be given to any person who may apprehend this and negro ex. of the State; and fifty dollars if apprehended in this State outside of Ripley county, or $25 if taken in Ripley county.

APOS TUCKER.

In 1850, Harriet was successful in helping Mary and her children flee from Maryland to Pennsylvania. Harriet was now a conductor on the Underground Railroad. As such, she knew the routes to take and the locations of safe houses.

Being a conductor on the Underground Railroad was a dangerous job. The journeys were difficult and the work was against the law. At one time, a reward of $40,000 was offered for Harriet's capture. But she would not be stopped.

By the end of her career as a conductor, Harriet had made 19 trips to the South to help slaves escape. She had freed about 300 slaves, including her parents and other family members.

By 1860, the **abolition movement** was well established. The country elected Abraham Lincoln as its president. Lincoln declared himself against the expansion of slavery into the new territories. His election caused 11 pro-slavery states to withdraw from the United States. In 1861, the **Civil War** broke out. Harriet Tubman quickly got involved in the war. She acted as a spy for the Northern army, helped nurse wounded soldiers, and continued her efforts to bring enslaved African Americans to freedom.

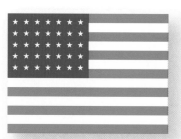

Union flag

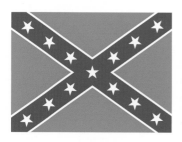

Confederate flag

⚓Lincoln's opposition to the expansion of slavery into the new territories led to the outbreak of war in 1861.

The war ended in 1865 with a Union victory. Soon after, an **amendment** to the U.S. Constitution outlawing slavery was passed. Tubman returned to her home in Auburn, New York, where she had moved in 1857. Even there she continued helping people. She provided food and shelter for the poor.

In 1896 she bought a house that 12 years later she turned into a home for sick and needy African Americans. It was here that Tubman spent her last few years. She died in 1913, but the tireless work she did to help others has had a lasting effect on society.

This undated cartoon illustration shows slave owner George Shelby giving freedom to his slaves. The Thirteenth Amendment abolished slavery.

Susan B. Anthony

1820 - 1906

➤State of Massachusetts◄

Adams,
Massachusetts

Susan B. Anthony knew it was unfair to deny women the right to vote. She spent her life fighting to change the law and give women fair treatment.

Susan Brownell Anthony was born on February 15, 1820, in Adams, Massachusetts. Her father was a **Quaker**. In a time when men were generally thought to be smarter and more important than women, Quakers treated women and men as equals.

Young Susan began attending school when her family moved to New York in 1826. When her father found out that the girls were not being taught long division, he decided to start his own school. In that school, girls and boys would learn the same things.

In 1837, Susan B. Anthony went away to boarding school. The experience was not a happy one. However, while she was there she met Lucretia Mott. Mott believed that it was important to help others. She also believed that slavery was wrong. Her views had an influence on young Susan.

Anthony became a teacher and taught school from 1839 to 1849. During that time she was paid less than male teachers. At teachers' meetings, she noticed how women were forced to sit in the back and be silent. It didn't take long for her to become interested in women's rights.

At the same time, this outspoken young woman became involved in the fight against slavery. She also joined the fight against drinking alcohol, known as the Temperance Movement.

⬇ Temperance Movement members demonstrated in front of places where men gathered to drink.

IT'S A FACT

Elizabeth Cady Stanton lived from 1815 to 1902. She and Lucretia Mott organized the first women's rights conference. There, Elizabeth wrote the Declaration of Sentiments. It said that women had the right to own property, to have freedom to speak freely, and to vote.

In 1851, Anthony met another champion of women's rights—Elizabeth Cady Stanton. Stanton had been working for women's rights for several years. Although many people agreed that women should be equal to men, others were not willing to give women the right to vote. Together, Anthony, Stanton, and Mott continued to fight for women's rights.

During the 1850s, Anthony continued to work in the movement against slavery. The **abolitionists** respected her work for women's rights and asked her to help them. She organized anti-slavery meetings and helped slaves escape to freedom through the Underground Railroad. Her work with the Underground Railroad brought her into contact with Harriet Tubman.

Anthony kept up her work in the Temperance Movement, too. During the time she was involved in this movement and in the anti-slavery movement, she experienced **discrimination** for being a woman. She wasn't allowed to speak at temperance meetings or abolition meetings. Women weren't supposed to speak in public.

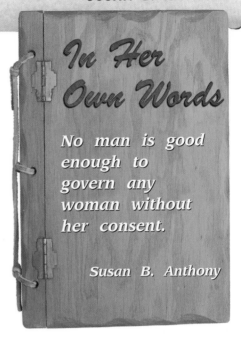

In Her Own Words

No man is good enough to govern any woman without her consent.

Susan B. Anthony

⚘Wendell Phillips, a famous abolitionist, delivers an anti-slavery speech in Boston, Massachusetts, on April 11, 1851.

These experiences made Anthony even more aware that women had little power in society. So she began to focus more of her efforts on women's rights.

Anthony and Stanton both believed that in order for women to get more power, married women had to have the right to own property. They worked hard to get this right for women. In 1860, the Married Women's Property Act was passed in New York State. Although this was an important victory, women still didn't have the right to vote.

Susan B. Anthony and Elizabeth Cady Stanton worked hard to guarantee women the right to vote.

In 1861, the Civil War began. While the fighting went on, the state of New York cancelled most of the Married Women's Property Act.

At the end of the war, the Thirteenth Amendment was passed. This amendment outlawed slavery. Anthony then turned all her attention to winning the right to vote for women.

Soon after, the Fifteenth Amendment was passed. This amendment gave the right to vote to African American men. All women were still denied the right to vote.

Point

Write About It

The U.S. Constitution in its original form did not give all people the right to vote. Some people had to fight very hard for that right. Why do you think this was so? Write down your thoughts.

After the Civil War, women began to speak up more about wanting the right to vote.

IT'S A FACT

In 1874, the U.S. Supreme Court ruled that it was the right of individual states to determine who could vote. That meant each state could decide whether or not women could vote.

In 1872, Anthony organized a group of women in New York State to **register** and vote. On November 5, 1872, 16 women—including Anthony—voted in an election for the president of the United States.

About three weeks later, the women were arrested. Although they had managed to register, it was still against the law for women to vote. Anthony was put on trial, found guilty, and fined $100. She refused to pay, but was never sent to prison.

The resolution giving women the right to vote was approved by Congress and sent to the states for ratification in 1918. It became the Nineteenth Amendment to the U.S. Constitution in 1920. ⚲

Susan B. Anthony kept fighting to change the U.S. Constitution. She did live to see women begin to "get the vote." During the 1890s, Wyoming, Utah, Colorado, and Idaho allowed women to vote. Sadly, however, she died before a constitutional amendment giving women the right to vote was passed.

League of Women Voters

After the passage of the Nineteenth Amendment, women were encouraged to exercise their legal right to vote.

On August 26, 1920, the Nineteenth Amendment to the U.S. Constitution was passed. Women across the country could now vote! Susan B. Anthony's fight for what she knew was right had finally paid off.

As a result of the Nineteenth Amendment, women all over the United States had the right to vote.

Eleanor Roosevelt

1884 - 1962

⟩State of New York⟨

New York City,
New York

Eleanor Roosevelt was one of the most famous First Ladies of the United States. She was a champion of the rights of women, children, and African Americans.

Anna Eleanor Roosevelt was born on October 11, 1884, in New York City. Although her family was rich, life wasn't easy for Eleanor, as she was called. A shy, serious little girl, she did not have much self-confidence.

In 1892, when young Eleanor was only eight years old, her mother died. Young Eleanor and her brothers went to live with their grandmother. Two years later, her father died.

Although she was surrounded by family at her grandmother's home, she still felt lonely. When she was 15, she was sent to a school in England. There her life began to improve.

Roosevelt was able to make friends quickly. People liked her because she was kind and caring. She was also a very smart young woman. It was not long before she became the top student at the school.

Young Eleanor, shown here with her horse, described herself as "tall, very thin, and very shy."

Eleanor as a young lady

Roosevelt finished school in 1902 and went back to New York. She was 18, and her family expected her to socialize and meet a husband. She made new friends, but she still missed her old school friends.

Roosevelt joined the Junior League, a group of women who put their time and energy into helping people. There she had a chance to do things she considered worthwhile. She visited areas in New York City where she taught classes to poor children. She visited with women and children who worked in **sweatshops** and helped out as best she could. For her, it was important to help people.

This sweatshop in New York City employed women for long hours in unhealthy conditions at low pay.

Around this time, Eleanor Roosevelt met a distant cousin whom she hadn't seen in many years. His name was Franklin Roosevelt. Eleanor and Franklin were married in 1905.

Eleanor Roosevelt was soon busy raising a family while Franklin Roosevelt was building a career in politics. In 1913, he became Assistant Secretary of the Navy for the United States. This job was in Washington, D.C., so the family moved there.

Franklin Roosevelt ran for vice president in 1920. His party lost. But Eleanor Roosevelt was able to vote for him because women had finally won the right to vote!

IT'S A FACT

Eleanor was becoming an activist for women's rights. Franklin suggested that she and her co-workers build a cottage near Val-Kill Stream on his family's property in New York. It would be a place where they could meet and do their political work. Later, the women opened a small furniture factory on the grounds of Val-Kill that employed local people.

In 1917, the United States became involved in World War I. Eleanor (in the center) helped out by working for the Red Cross.

After Franklin Roosevelt lost the election, the family moved back to New York. In 1921, he became ill with polio. The disease left him unable to walk without the help of heavy leg braces.

In 1928, Franklin Roosevelt was elected governor of New York. He served in this position until 1932.

In 1932, Franklin Roosevelt was elected president of the United States. Because it was so difficult for him to walk, Eleanor Roosevelt traveled around the country and made speeches for him. The country was in the middle of the **Great Depression**. Many people were out of work and did not have enough money for food and housing. Eleanor used her role as First Lady to speak out about the needs of women and children.

🎋 Eleanor was a champion of the unemployed. Here she visits with unemployed women at Bear Mountain Camp in New York.

Eleanor gave speeches around the country and also talked to the nation on the radio. She wrote a newspaper column. She was the first First Lady to do these things!

Franklin Roosevelt was elected president three more times, in 1936, 1940, and 1944. After the United States entered World War II in 1941, Eleanor continued her humanitarian work. She fought against putting Japanese Americans in **internment camps**. She tried to get a bill passed in Congress that would help German Jewish children enter the United States to escape the war in Germany.

Not long after his election for a fourth term as president, Franklin Roosevelt died in April 1945. Because she was no longer First Lady, Eleanor moved to Val-Kill, where she continued her work.

⚓ Eleanor traveled all over the world during World War II to visit soldiers.

A few weeks later, Eleanor was chosen by the new president, Harry S. Truman, to attend the first meeting of the United Nations. World War II had left many children in Europe homeless. Eleanor became involved in the United Nations International Children's Emergency Fund, or UNICEF, helping find homes for the children.

In 1946, Eleanor was elected head of the United Nations Commission on Human Rights. There she directed the writing of the Universal Declaration of Human Rights. This declaration said that people everywhere in the world must have the same rights, such as freedom from slavery, equal pay for equal work, and freedom of speech. Its approval was probably one of Eleanor's proudest moments.

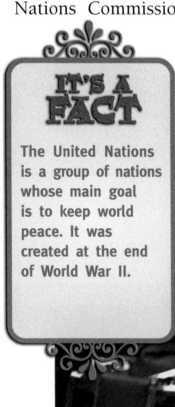

IT'S A FACT

The United Nations is a group of nations whose main goal is to keep world peace. It was created at the end of World War II.

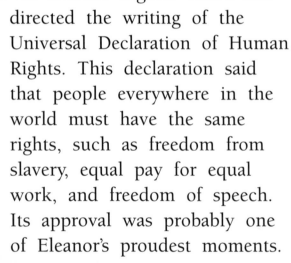

After her triumph at the United Nations, Eleanor continued to visit countries around the world. Everywhere she went, people loved her.

Eleanor continued to work and travel until her death in 1962. The world was saddened by the loss of this respected woman. She had spent her life helping other people obtain a better life.

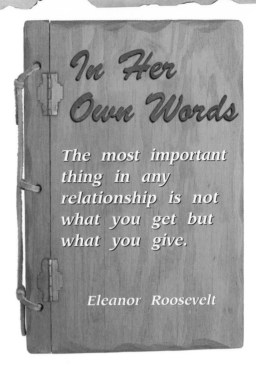

In Her Own Words

The most important thing in any relationship is not what you get but what you give.

Eleanor Roosevelt

Conclusion

arriet Tubman, Susan B. Anthony, and Eleanor Roosevelt were great humanitarians and activists. Each one helped people, making the world a better place.

Harriet Tubman risked her life again and again to help free enslaved African Americans. Susan B. Anthony spent her life working to get women the right to vote. Eleanor Roosevelt worked for the rights of people around the world.

✔ Point

Reread

Reread the words of Harriet Tubman, Susan B. Anthony, and Eleanor Roosevelt on pages 8, 17, and 29. What conclusion(s) can you draw about these women from their words?

Glossary

abolition movement	(ab-uh-LIH-shun MOOV-ment) a group of people working to end slavery (page 12)
abolitionist	(ab-uh-LIH-shun-ist) a person who works to end slavery (page 16)
activist	(AK-tih-vist) a person who engages in action for or against an issue (page 2)
amendment	(uh-MEND-ment) a change to the original U.S. Constitution (page 13)
Civil War	(CIH-vil WAR) a war in which states in the North fought against states in the South (1861–1865) (page 12)
conductor	(kon-DUKT-or) a person who guided slaves to freedom on the Underground Railroad (page 9)
discrimination	(DIH-skrim-ih-NAY-shun) treating people differently based on their skin color, religion, or gender (page 17)
Great Depression	(GRAYT dee-PREH-shun) a time when businesses did poorly and many people had little or no money (1929–1939) (page 26)
humanitarian	(hyoo-man-ih-TARE-ee-uhn) a person who works to better the lives of others (page 2)
injustice	(in-JUH-stiss) something that is unfair (page 2)
internment camp	(in-TERN-ment KAMP) a place where people are confined or imprisoned (page 27)
Quaker	(KWAY-kur) a member of a religious group, the Society of Friends, who believes in humanitarianism and works for peace (page 14)
register	(REH-jih-stur) to sign up to vote (page 20)
sweatshop	(SWET-shop) a place where people work for long hours and low pay under unhealthy conditions (page 24)
Underground Railroad	(UN-dur-grownd RAYL-rode) the system of escape routes that helped bring slaves to freedom (page 9)

Index